Ten Simple Rules for Being a Better Parent in a World Turned Upside Down

Ten Simple Rules
for Being a
Better Parent
in a World Turned Upside Down

*A handbook to help parents do a better job
starting today*

John D. McPherson Jr.

Mill City Press
Minneapolis, MN

Mill City Press, Inc.
212 3rd Avenue North, Suite 290
Minneapolis, MN 55401
612.455.2294
www.millcitypublishing.com

ISBN - 978-1-936107-22-3
ISBN - 1-936107-22-8
LCCN - 2009943413

Cover Design and Typeset by Sophie Chi

Printed in the United States of America

CONTENTS

To Mom and Dad

INTRODUCTION

There are many crises demanding our attention today. The world does indeed seem to have turned upside down. You have to look hard to find positives today, while problems fly at us from all directions. There is one crisis, however, that is getting far less attention than what the facts demand. It cuts so straight to our core that even if we solve all the others but leave this one unaddressed, the prospects of our society succeeding are slim. We can fix all the money problems, all the environmental problems, and all the political problems, but if we don't fix this problem our foundation will continue to be weak. It will continue to be weak because this crisis is about what type of people our children will turn out to be. This crisis is about how we've lost our ability to be good parents.

The evidence is all around us, but we have trouble attributing these problems to the root cause of poor parenting. We—for the first time—are concerned that the generations that follow will be in worse shape than we are. This is a very troubling development, and we have to honestly ask ourselves why we feel this way. A common answer places the blame on all of the challenges and issues that face our society today. Make no mistake, the challenges and issues facing our society are daunting, but all of them can be overcome if that society is well-educated, healthy, and dynamic. The root cause of our concern is we have not done our job in preparing our children for the challenges ahead, and that fact is feeding our anxiety about their future. Unfortunately, those feelings of anxiety are well founded. The sobering reality is that the next generation is not well educated, healthy, or dynamic. We have not taught our children how to learn, work, behave, or take care of themselves.

When you look at the data on learning, working, behaving, and being healthy, it is astonishing. Parents largely have surrendered their role in teaching their children solely to the schools, which have become overwhelmed and the results show it. Between 1995 and 2003, the US dropped two spots in the TIMSS International Math Study from sixth to eighth for those countries participating in both studies for fourth-graders. In science, the US has gone from second to fifth (1). When it comes to literacy, the US basically treaded water between 2001 and 2006, while fourteen other countries improved their scores (2). This trend explains the government's decision to turn public education into an endless loop of standardized tests just to keep up with the rest of the world. Unfortunately, these efforts have not succeeded, as demonstrated by the fact that the average 2009 SAT reading score was the same as it was in 1994. Our initial reaction is to blame this on the schools, when in fact parents need to look in the mirror and ask themselves what they are doing to ensure that their children are prepared to learn when they leave the house in the morning.

In addition to not performing well at school, our children are also not behaving very well there or at any other place. Again, parents currently point the finger at the schools when they need to be looking at their own behavior. According to a 2002 study done by Public Agenda, Americans say that disrespect, lack of consideration, and rudeness are serious, pervasive problems that affect them on a personal level. Eight in ten Americans say a lack of respect and courtesy is a serious problem, with six in ten saying things have become worse in recent years. A surprising 41 percent admit that they're part of the problem and sometimes behave badly themselves. Americans are particularly concerned about the discourteous and disrespectful conduct of children, and they hold parents primarily responsible for this phenomenon. People say that too many parents don't invest the energy needed to teach their children good behavior, and that too often they fail to set a good example themselves (3).

When it comes to work, our young people are not entering the workforce with the skills and work ethic necessary to compensate for their surly attitudes. According to a 2006 study, the incoming Y generation was sorely lacking in much-needed workplace skills—both basic academic and more advanced skills. The study reflects employers' growing frustrations over the preparedness of new entrants to the workforce. More than 40 percent of surveyed employers said incoming high school graduates hired are deficiently prepared for the entry-level jobs they fill and lack the basic skills in reading comprehension, writing, and math, which many respondents say were needed for successful job performance. Also, nearly three-quarters of survey participants (70 percent) cite deficiencies among incoming high school graduates in "applied" skills, such as professionalism and work ethic, defined as "demonstrating personal accountability, effective work habits, punctuality, working productively with others, time and workload management" (4). This situation was bad enough when our economy was cruising along with a 5 percent unemployment rate and service jobs galore, but that economy is gone now. Our children will have to compete for fewer, more demanding jobs, and they are not prepared to do so.

The most troubling statistics of all, however, show that as a society we are slowly killing our children. According to the Centers for Disease Control and Prevention, from 1980 to 2004 the prevalence of overweight children and adolescents has increased alarmingly. For children aged 2–5 years, prevalence increased from 5 percent to 13.9 percent; for those aged 6–11 years, prevalence increased from 6.5 percent to 18.8 percent; and for those aged 12–19 years, prevalence increased from 5 percent to 17.4 percent (5). In the past we didn't consider being overweight a risk for children, but that is not the case now. Overweight children and adolescents are more likely to have risk factors associated with cardiovascular disease than are other children and adolescents (6). The incidents of Type 2 Diabetes among adolescents, though still not high, has increased by a factor of more than ten in the past two decades and may now exceed that of Type 1 Diabetes among black and Hispanic adolescents. Fatty liver associated with excessive weight, unrecognized in the pediatric literature before 1980, today occurs in about one in three obese children. Other obesity-related complications affecting virtually every organ—ranging from crippling orthopedic problems to sleep apnea—are being diagnosed with increasing frequency in children. There is also a heavy psycho-social toll, as obese children tend to be socially isolated and have high rates of disordered eating, anxiety, and depression (7). Most importantly, we are finding now that this is not a problem children grow out of, because overweight children and adolescents are more likely to become obese adults. One study found that approximately 80 percent of children who were overweight at aged 10–15 years were obese adults at age 25 years. There is now also clear evidence that higher Body Mass Index (BMI) during childhood is associated with an increased risk of coronary heart disease in adulthood (8).

In short, we are creating a selfish, rude, uneducated society that, on top of all that, is digging itself an early grave. An important point to make is this is not a problem associated with class, economic status, or race. While it is true that the more serious problems are more prevalent in the economically disadvantaged segments of our society, the issue of poor parenting, and the results, is affecting the kids coming out the affluent segments of society as well. Money is not required to be a good parent, and the presence of money certainly is no substitute for good parenting. We also have to accept that the turmoil our economy is experiencing and will continue to experience is only going to make things more difficult. There is no cavalry coming over the hill with bags of money to spread around, so we are all going to have to adapt and play the hand we have been dealt.

So, how did we get here?

First, society today has many more positive dynamics in play than negative. However, not every dynamic is positive. We all have to acknowledge and accept that there are negative dynamics too. These negative dynamics are the root cause for most of society's problems. This is no revelation, but the trick is to accurately identify these dynamics, particularly as they relate to parenting.

To explain why parenting has suffered over the past forty years I've identified four negative dynamics that have had a strong influence on society and, therefore, a strong influence on how we parent. Although the "blame game" has become a national sport, I do not assign blame for these negative dynamics to any person or group other than society as a whole. Figuring that all out would be another book much longer than this one. This book is about what to do about the issues caused by these dynamics, not what caused them. Also, one of the reasons we play the blame game is to immediately deflect attention from the actual problem, so let's not fall into that trap. As parents we need to look beyond who is at fault and accept responsibility for doing something about it, and that is what this book is about.

A Sense of Entitlement:

Over the last forty years we have built a proud record of facing the injustices that have tormented our society and can honestly say we've made things better. There is a fine line, however, between true injustice and perceived injustice. An issue in our society today is that more and more people see the things that those before them worked hard to acquire or achieve and believe that they too should also have those things, but without the work. These people believe they are entitled to these things. When these people don't get these things, it can cause anger and resentment. For example, early in my professional career I attended one of those sales-skills boot camps someplace in the Georgia woods. The attendees were broken up into groups of four, and then we went through a couple of days of role-playing, with all the team members giving honest feedback on how each individual did. I was in a group with one of the company's top salespeople, so it was a very dynamic and productive group. However, after two days we all were called into an office and told there was a problem. We were told that one individual in the group had complained that the rest of the group was being too critical about this individual's performance because we were biased against this individual. This confused me greatly, because I was by far the weakest in the group and was taking the brunt of the criticism. It became apparent, though, that this person just didn't like to be critiqued and felt they should be given the course-completion certificate without having to actually work to improve their sales skills. The fact that it wasn't happening meant there was a problem, and that problem was that the rest of the group was being unfair. This is just one example, and I can cite dozens more that I've encountered in my lifetime, which I'm sure anyone reading this book can do as well. It is also important to accept that this dynamic has nothing to do with race or gender…we all own this one.

A perfect example of this dynamic at work today is our crumpled economy. Our economy was brought to the brink of collapse because people stopped paying mortgages when a huge part of the economy depended on people paying their mortgages. The list of people and institutions responsible for these risky mortgage loans being made is long and complicated, but the reason the loans were made is very simple: people felt entitled to a lifestyle beyond their means and were willing to roll the dice to get it. The people in charge should have prevented this mess from getting out of control, but our sense of entitlement to the big house and flat-screen TV fueled the fire. Through the 1980s and 1990s, total consumer debt ran between 50 percent and 70 percent of GDP. By 2008, however, it was running close to 100 percent, meaning we owed as much money in debt as the entire US economy generated in a year (9). That is a lot of money that either has to be paid back or defaulted on, and the consequences of that default will be felt for generations. Another example of this has been the explosion of gambling over the last thirty years. The only people who make money in gambling are the people running the games. If you gamble, you lose—period. Some people might get huffy about this statement, but those sparkling Las Vegas palaces were built on the losses of the average gambler, not the winnings. The fact that states run lotteries is proof enough. States run lotteries to make money. This means they take in more than they pay out, which means you lose. A friend of ours once said lotteries were simply a tax for people who can't do math. This is common sense, but gambling has boomed in the last thirty years because people feel entitled to a life they can't afford and therefore convince themselves their number will come up. People who run these games have recognized this and made billions. When you look at the advertising put out by state lotteries, you see that they've found the magic words to tap into this sense of entitlement. While this is a problem with all economic segments of society, it is a huge problem for those who can least afford it. A study done to combat the Arkansas state lottery found that lottery players with incomes below $10,000 spend more than any other income group on the lottery, an estimated $597 per year (10).

Another troubling example of this dynamic is the fact that we now believe we are entitled to having children, but on our terms. A 2005 study showed that out-of-wedlock births in the United States climbed to an all-time high, accounting for nearly four in ten babies born. While out-of-wedlock births have long been associated with teen mothers, the teen birthrate actually dropped to the lowest level on record. Instead, births among unwed mothers rose most dramatically among women in their 20s (11). This means women are making the conscious choice to have children without getting married because they feel they are entitled to having children and don't feel they need to do the work of building a family first. This is not a condemnation of single mothers. Most don't choose to be in that category, and many do a fantastic job. Again, common sense tells us that parenting is at least a two-person job, so for people to take on such a task intentionally by themselves means they are only seeing the good stuff and none of the hard, hard work required to raise a child effectively.

The affect of this dynamic on our children is profound. Besides saddling them with a debt that will have a direct influence on their standard of living, we are installing a mind-set that will be a roadblock to their success. By our own actions we are teaching our children to expect things to be handed to them and react when it doesn't happen. Children largely see the world through their parents' eyes, so if they see Mom or Dad with a chip on their shoulders, they are going to put one on their shoulder too, and starting life with a chip on your shoulder can lead to a lot of disappointment, frustration, and bad decisions. If we continue to let that happen, then we do great damage to a child's sense of independence and responsibility for their own actions, which are the cornerstones for future success. A 2006 study found that 83 percent of respondents strongly or somewhat agreed that America's youth feel more entitled compared to ten years ago (12).

Matt Berkley, a writer in St. Louis, put it best when he said, "We're surprised we have to work for our money. We want the corner office right away" (13). When you take into account what our economy is going to look like over the next twenty years, this attitude is chilling. The old economy may have had corner offices to be handed out, but the new economy needs someone to build them, and the entitlement mind-set has to change for that to happen.

Society of Convenience:

In the first half of the twentieth century, a generation managed to create a society better than they or anyone had seen before. Ironically, this achievement has become a siren singing from the rocks. Since we now can live our lives eating at the drive-through and never leaving the couch, we have created a society where many among us aren't willing or able to take care of themselves. We now take for granted so many things that through the generations required so much effort to have and achieve, we've lost track of what the human experience truly is. The number of meals eaten away from home has more than doubled in less than thirty years. In 1978, 16 percent of meals were eaten away from home; it is now more than 30 percent. Approximately 40 percent of the food budget is now spent on food that is eaten outside the home (14). In 1960, there were 52 million television sets in American homes. In 2006 there were 285 million, when the average American home actually crossed the threshold of having more television sets than people (15). In 1960 there were .85 motor vehicles for every driver; now there is 1.18 for every driver (16).

These "advancements" really mean we can now get though our lives without learning how to cook, carry on a conversation, or use our feet to get from one place to another. The problem with this is that it's not what people were designed for. The blueprint calls for a social and active lifestyle. In a troubled world, we need to be light on our feet, have a clear eye, and be resourceful. In the world of the next fifty years our children need to be even sharper, and the opposite is happening. We need to be teaching our children how to take care of themselves, not how to order pizza while watching *American Idol* and Twittering the whole experience.

Wanting to Be Our Kids' Friends:

Over the course of the last twenty years the need and desire to be our children's friends has outpaced the understanding that we first need to be their parents. We can see this by an increasing reluctance among parents to be "the bad guy" and an increase in avoidance of any sort of conflict or discipline. In our defense, some of us experienced a very heavy hand from our parents that was, at best, counterproductive and, at worst, abusive. We therefore go to extremes to not repeat our own negative experiences. Some feel very overwhelmed by the task and responsibility, so they just "go along to get along." For some it's very important to stay young, so they choose to act young and recast their relationships with their children at more of a peer level. Others feel quite strongly that it isn't their place to set rules for another human being. All of this adds up to a large number of families where the roles of parent and child have been blended to a degree.

This is a problem because blurring the lines between parent and friend means the important lines don't get drawn for our children. If parents aren't willing to do the parenting job, who will? If you drive a car across a bridge without guardrails, sooner or later that car is going over the side, and it is the same way with children.

Unwillingness to Sacrifice:

The generation that built our Society of Convenience did so in part to ensure their kids wouldn't have to make the same sacrifices they did. This noble effort has, unfortunately, backfired to a certain extent. Today we have taken the fact that we don't have to make the same sacrifices our parents and grandparents made and turned it into an unwillingness to make *any* sacrifices. A study done by Oxford University's Institute on Aging showed that less than 10 percent of people surveyed said they want to pass on money to their children when they go, while 60 percent want their legacy to be their "outlook on life." While there are many legitimate reasons for this, and there is nothing wrong with passing on a positive outlook, it is an indicator of a change in parental understanding of what parents' responsibilities are to their children, and one of those responsibilities is sacrificing something of theirs to give to their children. When it comes to money, parents—rich or poor—have historically shown their commitment and dedication by the act of ensuring there was something that could be handed down to their children. The most important thing here is what that devotion has meant, not the money. Another example comes from a 2002 study done by Monster.com that found half of US jobseekers were willing to relocate for a new job, with their career and education levels directly proportionate to their mobility (17). You'll notice there is no mention of family here. I had a colleague who moved for a great career opportunity but had a dark cloud hanging over his head. When I asked why, he confessed that while the move was great for him on a personal level, it was devastating for his daughter, who was entering her last year of high school when the move occurred.

The issue here is, since we have focused so much on what this wonderful world can provide us, we've failed to recognize that the successful development of a child requires the act of putting their needs before our own. We've lost sight of the fact that the act of sacrificing on a parent's part is far more valuable than any results that come from avoiding sacrifice. The father who never misses a game, even when he is coming off a double shift, will win out over the dad who always has an important meeting but comes home with gifts to make up for it. Human nature tells us when someone is doing something for themselves as opposed to doing something for others, and children are indeed human. Knowing that someone is willing to sacrifice for them not only provides children a comfort that can't be bought but teaches a lesson that can't be learned in any school.

These are the negative dynamics affecting how we parent, which this book is intended to counter with ten simple rules. Who am I to do this? Simply put, I'm a parent who cares about being a good parent and who has been paying attention. I am not a researcher, professor, or therapist; I am a day-to-day parent. I have made these observations and come to these conclusions over the past few years based on three influences.

First, what I learned—both at the time and later in life—from my own parents and how they raised their children. I am a tail-end baby-boomer born in 1963, so my parents were of the generation that went through both the Great Depression and World War II. This "Greatest Generation" has gotten a lot of attention in the past few years due to the amazing trials they had to endure and because there aren't many of them left. For me, the generation of my parents is actually the generation of my peers' grandparents when we would meet families with kids the same age. My sister and I were therefore directly influenced by the principles, values, and honor system that carried that generation through experiences that, quite frankly, people today can hardly fathom. At the writing of this book, our economy has officially tanked, with unemployment climbing toward double digits. I am contributing to this increase because I lost my job with a company for which I worked for eighteen years. This is something no one under the age of 65 has ever seen, but at the height of the Great Depression unemployment was over 20 percent for three straight years and over 15 percent for eight out of nine years. Also, we are rightly concerned that over 4,000 US soldiers have given their lives in Iraq since 2003, but in 1945 three times that many died in three months taking the island of Okinawa. The principles, values, and honor system forged by these experiences are what created the character of my parents' generation, and it is this character that I have drawn from my parents and am trying to pass on to my children. My father was, like the rest of us, far from perfect, but in the forty years I knew him I can safely say I never saw him do a single dishonest thing.

Second, my mother-in-law has had a great influence on my outlook on parenting. She is living proof that single parents can do a fantastic job of raising kids and can do it with grace. A large part of what is in this book has come from the simple yet firm standards and principles she stood by through the very challenging experience of raising two children on her own.

Third, as luck would have it, I have followed the same path as my parents and first started a family when I hit my 40s. This has given me the opportunity to observe a great number of parenting styles and outcomes before being thrown into the fire myself. It has also allowed me to be a parent as a much more mature person than I was in my 20s or, according to my wife, my 30s. The combination of these three things has led me to the realization that we as a society have lost our ability to be good parents, and this painful but clear fact has to be addressed. Those parenting styles and outcomes I observed, combined with what I know from my own experience, have led me to shine a light on the problem as I see it and offer a simple set of tried-and-true rules to help parents do a better job.

If there is still any lingering doubt about my assertions, let's look at what happened in Nebraska in 2008. Nebraska was one of the last states to implement a "Safe Haven" law designed to allow parents of newborn babies to leave their unwanted infants with authorities without being prosecuted. The reasoning for such a law is, if someone has a newborn and cannot deal with it, it's better to have them leave the baby at the hospital rather than on a street corner or worse. Nebraska, however, failed to include an age limit in the law. As a result, over thirty children ranging from age 5 to age 17 were pushed out of the car by their parents onto the state of Nebraska. Children were even driven from Florida and California to be dropped off. Now, I am not making the claim that the fact that these parents did this proves my point. In many cases this may have been the best option available. However, the fact that it came to this for these parents proves my point. I am confident that these parents never expected to be in this position, but since the parenting job didn't get done right, this is where they found themselves. I am sure their intentions were good from the start, but you have to know what to be good at as a parent in order to be a successful parent.

My goal with this book, therefore, is to help parents understand what things are important to be good at and make simple, relevant, and easy-to-remember recommendations on how to be good at those things. I've broken it down into ten simple rules and, in David Letterman fashion, we will count them down from number ten to number one.

RULE #10

It's Not about You Anymore

Something I see often is parents saying one thing but doing another when it comes to making a decision between what they want for themselves and what's best for their children. If you ask any parent what is the most important thing to them, they will answer "My kids" almost instantaneously. While I truly think that people believe this in their heart, they often don't act that way. They talk the talk but don't walk the walk. When it comes down to making this type of decision, the thing that is important to the parent often ends up taking priority over what is in the children's best interest. To be blunt, parents in certain situations act selfishly and then try to rationalize it. Here are some examples, some hypothetical and some not. First I'll list the examples, and then I'll point out where not focusing on what is in the child's best interest in each can cause problems.

Example 1: A parent makes time every week to do something important to him or her. Whether it is going out with friends to let off a little steam, a card game, scrapbooking, or playing softball, that activity will take place every week come rain or shine.

Example 2: Every night when Dad comes home he has a scowl on his face and only wants to read the paper or watch the ballgame. Work has been hell, and he needs his "cave time," as my wife would say.

Example 3: A parent has a poor relationship with one of their children's grandparents and minimizes the amount of time the extended family spends together.

Example 4: A parent pulls their child from a particular school because they have an issue with a teacher, administrator, or finds that the parking-lot gossip mob has turned on them.

Example 5: A parent insists their child take up a sport or activity that the parent did when they were a child and insists they continue to do it even if the child says they don't like it.

Example 6: Dad comes home one day with a big smile on his face and a bright, shiny new Daddy Toy in tow. Sure, it cost a small bucket of money, but it is something he's always dreamed of.

Example 7: Here's one I touched on in the introduction. A father of a high school junior has worked his entire career to achieve a certain position, and now that position is being offered to him and he takes it. This promotion, however, will require the family to relocate and his daughter to attend a new school for her final year of high school.

Some of these might give you a twinge, and some might seem perfectly fine, but all of them do one thing: show the child that some things are more important to you than they are.

In our first example, the child knows there is something in their parents' life that they like doing more than spending time with them. Children understand that Mommy and Daddy need Mommy and Daddy time, but when it is rigid and uncompromising, the child knows which is more important. In the second example, the child feels unwanted. In the third example, the child knows it's more important to his or her parent that they be spared an awkward couple of hours than it is for the child to spend time with their grandma or grandpa. In the forth example, the child knows the parent's wishes matter more than the fact they like the school and all their friends are there. In the next example, the child can't understand why it is so important to Mom or Dad that they play tennis when they would rather be in dance. In Example 6, Daddy has a new expensive toy, but the children don't. And in our last example, the child knows that her father's career is worth making her life a living hell. If you doubt this, think back to what it would have been like to be the new kid for your senior year in high school. The only time this worked out was in the movie *Footloose*.

Now some of these observations may seem overly severe from your perspective, but that's from your perspective. Take a deep breath and look at each one of these from a child's perspective. Even when there are good reasons for these things to happen, it's tough on the child. In the third example there may be some really good reasons why Mom and Grandma shouldn't be in the same room, and in the last example sometimes job relocations aren't optional. For the child the result is the same, however. Their needs have been made secondary, and they know it. When these things can't be avoided, the child needs to be told that. The purpose of this rule, however, is to help parents avoid "unforced errors," as they say in tennis, because these things have a negative impact on children. They result in anger and resentment from the child and, most importantly, leave the child questioning whether or not they are loved. Again, this may seem harsh, but there is little about being selfish when dealing with your children that results in good. We need to remember the definition of *selfish* is, "Concerned excessively or exclusively with oneself: seeking or concentrating on one's own advantage, pleasure, or well-being without regard for others."

So, how do we avoid this? For those things that do have an impact, we need to simply ask ourselves the question, "Who am I doing this for?" If the answer comes back, at least partially, that you are doing it for your children, then you are on the right track. If not, then you need to evaluate it, make sure you have the balance right and then possibly rethink it.

If we apply this to our first example, you will know if your "me time" is becoming an issue because it will be pointed out to you. If no one ever says anything, you have the balance right. A night out with the girls or a card game once every two months, for example, isn't going to cause a problem and is probably quite healthy. However, if you get that look from your child or, even worse, that other look from your spouse, then you need to scale back. Even if you do have the balance right, making a point of dropping what you were planning on doing once in a while to spend time with your child will be noticed and go a long, long way. You can also incorporate them into what you're doing, if at all possible. If it is something you love, then your child will probably like it too and think it's great you are sharing it.

In our second example, everyone needs quiet time as well as "me time," but the fact is *you* need to adapt, not your child. You may not want to jump in with your kids when you first walk through the door, but your kids are thrilled to see you, and if you push them off, they

are going to think it's because of them. Spend an extra
five minutes in the car or take a quick walk around the
block, so when you hit that front door you are ready.
Also, a special note for the working-outside-the-home
parent: you may have had a hard day, but the working-
inside-the-home-parent, who has been living with the
children all day, didn't fare much better. Diving right in
when you walk through the door makes you a hero all
the way around.

In our third example, if the grandparents aren't a threat
to your children's health and safety, then you have to
suck it up, put on a thin smile, and make sure your
children have these people in their lives. Remember, you
know lots of people, but children know very few adults
and even fewer who really care about them. Denying
them time with these people because you don't like to
spend time with them is selfish, plain and simple.

In our fourth example, all that should matter is whether
or not the school is the best place for the child to
develop at that point in their life. If the answer is yes,
then they should stay there regardless of any issues the
parent has with anyone. In the fifth example it's great to
make sure your child tries a variety of activities at least
once. Whether they do them again, however, should
be totally up to the child. There are two issues with
Example 6. First, adult toys are really expensive. Now,
if you are one of those very lucky people that are sitting
on a pile of money, then good for you. However, if you

are like the rest of us, then that money should be spent someplace else or saved. When little Billy can't go to camp because Daddy has motorcycle insurance to pay, that's a problem. Second, if you bought an expensive toy, you will probably want to spend lots of time with it, which brings us back to the first example.

In our last example, the look on the dad's face when he told me about the moment he realized what his daughter was going through said it all. He had been so focused on getting that job he didn't take a moment to put himself in his daughter's shoes. All the friends she had were gone. She knew nobody. Instead of her senior year of high school being remembered in a happy way, it would be the opposite. He was dead serious when he said he wished he could do it over and stay where they were. It would be one thing if the move had to happen to keep the job or make ends meet. This happens all the time and is a part of life. It is quite another, though, when it is voluntary and there is a choice. This concept all came together for me after a discussion I had with my father about why he stayed at the same company and almost the same job for thirty years. I was starting my career and expected to bounce around a lot, so I was curious why someone would stay in the same place for that long. He looked at me and asked if I liked living in our house while growing up. I didn't expect that and had to think about it. Once I did, it dawned on me that, yes, I really liked living in the same house from the first day I can remember until the age of 18. I knew every tree and every crack in the sidewalk, every neighbor knew my name, and I always knew where to go. No matter how long I live or where I end up, that house will always be home. So I told my dad that, yes, I did like it very much. He then said that's why he stayed at the same job for thirty years.

Once we accept the fact that by having kids we've taken on a responsibility much greater than just taking care of ourselves, we can start to see how to act. Our main responsibility is doing what's right for our children, not making ourselves happy. The true value here is, when you make these sacrifices, your children see that you are willing to give up a little of yourself and put some skin in the game. Children will see this and recognize it for what it is—a demonstration of your love and devotion. Children will not be truly happy unless they know in their hearts that their parents love them, so this is ground well worth covering. Bill Simmons, a sports columnist, demonstrated this brilliantly in one of his columns when he described waiting in a checkout line at Best Buy with a couple of DVDs in hand. Right in front of him was a kid excitedly holding *Grand Theft Auto IV*. Bill, though envious, stayed steady and completed his purchase of *Max and Ruby* for his children. If you are an adult and have ever watched five minutes of *Max and Ruby*, you know Mr. Simmons lived the rule that day.

Fortunately there is a light at the end of the tunnel in this harsh world of sacrifice I recommend. I've never seen a parent who had happy kids end up anything but happy and content themselves.

RULE #9

Be the Boss

A big stumbling block for parents today is discipline. Some choose to avoid it altogether, while others struggle with what is appropriate. What do you do from day to day, moment to moment? One of the things I've noticed over the last twenty years is that parents' confidence in discipline has suffered. Parents are tentative when it comes to exercising discipline and, when they do, they tend to bring a pretty weak effort. This has come about for a couple of reasons.

Guilt: Today parents, particularly working mothers, have to spend so much time outside of the home that we feel guilty about it. Therefore, we ease off the *No* pedal to try and balance things out. This needs to stop. Parents of the previous generation had plenty to be guilty about too, but they didn't hesitate to stand firm when it was the right thing to do.

Wanting to Be Our Child's Friend: We covered this in
the introduction, and it is a huge stumbling block when
it comes to discipline. There is no way you can assume
the role of friend without blurring the line between
parent and child. We are not colleagues, partners, fellow
travelers, or friends; we are parents and children.

The Parent Rules Have Changed: The rules on
parenting have changed dramatically over the past forty
years. This has been a very positive thing, but it is still
change. It therefore is sometimes hard to tell if you are
being a bit too hard on the kids. The tendency now is
to maybe err on the side of *Yes*, when in the past *No*
was the default. The issue here is that a bad *Yes* is much,
much worse than a bad *No*.

We need to look at this challenge not as one solely about
discipline but about leadership, because if you just try
to be the hard-ass without building a foundation where
your child trusts and respects you, it will end in failure.
Now, *leadership* can be an imposing word. One parent
said to me, "I don't want to save the world; I just want
to keep my kid out of trouble!" This being the case, let's
work with something that anyone who has ever held a
job understands. Parents need to be the boss. Actually,
I need to be more specific here. Parents need to be the
good boss, not that bad boss who screams and everyone
ignores. That bad boss only worries about being the
hard-ass and not a leader, so we are going to focus on

what we need to do to be a leader and good boss. Below are three tried-and-true attributes of a good boss:

Learn How to Say No: One of the most frustrating things about a bad boss is that even though they scream and yell, they don't like to make a decision. A good boss, on the other hand, is always willing to stand up and make the tough call. When it comes to parenting, this boils down to the very hard task of saying no to your child. This is certainly not a new concept. My mother-in-law would patiently wait for my wife to make her pitch when she was a little girl and then politely tell her no. The few times my wife attempted to continue the negotiations, her efforts were met with a much frostier and final no. My wife never tried a third time.

So, why is saying no important, when it is much easier and everyone is much happier when we say yes? The reason again is that children have to have boundaries set for them. If you don't set boundaries for your kids, it's not like they won't exist. It is human nature to find the boundary, and children are indeed humans. Setting these boundaries is not an occasional thing either. It is a constant, daily exercise as thoughts pop into your child's mind. Over the next few days, count how many times your child says, "Can I…?"

Every time we answer that question, we are setting a boundary, so it is something we have practice at. It gets tough, however, when that shining little face doesn't like the answer. From that point until the child is in his or her late 20s, life will be one long negotiation. If, like the bad boss, we don't step up and set the boundary when given the chance, then it will be set down the road in a much more painful way. Everyone who has ever had a boss that puts off the tough decisions knows that doing so only makes things worse down the line. It is the same way with children. We are doing our children a huge disservice if we don't do the boundary-setting for them while it's still relatively painless. That's what being a parent is all about.

So, how do we get the *No* train back on the track after years of giving in when we shouldn't have? This, of course, is much easier said than done. While this seems a daunting task, the most important question to remember is what best prepares your child to face the world ready to succeed come their eighteenth birthday? This is usually very different than what will make them happy today. A parent's primary responsibility is the former, not the latter. Just as a good boss needs to make decisions based on what is best for the business, parents need to make decisions on what is best for the child, not what will make them happy. Just as a good boss is responsible for the business running correctly, parents are legally responsible for the person our child is now and for the person they will be when they hit 18. We need to focus on preparing them to make the right decisions and to act the right way when they hit the doorstep of adulthood and become responsible for themselves.

Keeping this in mind, many a *Yes* should be a *No*, depending on the child. Can I go to Sally's house instead of doing the dishes? Can I get a tattoo? Can I stay out after 10:00 pm? A *Yes* to these would certainly bring a smile to our children's faces but do nothing to prepare them to be adults. In fact, saying yes can sometimes make that process harder. That tattoo you said yes to when the child was 17 is going to look pretty out of place when he or she turns 40. So how do we know when to say no? A good guide is to ask if what they want is age appropriate. This is a concept that has become lost in our culture because everyone wants to grow up right now. Girls should not have slogans written across their behinds; that is not age appropriate. Kids under the age of 17 should not be seeing R-rated movies; that is not age appropriate. Children under the age of 16 actually do not need to take cell phones to school; that is not age appropriate. Texting and talking on the phone to your friends is not the best way to spend the school day. If there is an emergency at school, then that is what the phone hanging from the wall in the office is for. If you are unsure, go with *No*. Remember, a bad *No* can be fixed pretty easily while a bad *Yes* can be a disaster.

Say What You Mean and Mean What You Say: Going back to the bad boss/good boss comparison, the bad boss is the one screaming and yelling when something doesn't get done, but the good boss never screams or yells, and everything actually does get done. How does that work? Well, the good boss has learned that their words need to matter, and so they only have to say them once. If the good boss says something should be done and it doesn't get done, the good boss makes sure there are consequences and everyone involved feels them. The next time the good boss says something needs to be done, it gets done. The bad boss just gets upset. The next time the bad boss says something needs to get done, everyone knows that if it doesn't get done, all that will happen is that the bad boss will get upset. Since no one really cares if the bad boss gets upset, then no one cares if the thing gets done or not. This translates directly to the parent/child relationship. When parents find themselves raising their voice or getting angry because they are being defied, we need to realize we are being defied because children don't care if we get angry or not. It's when we get so angry we actually do something that children will take notice. What we need to do is, as Theodore Roosevelt said, speak softly and carry a big stick, with that "big stick" being something the child cares about. Just like the good boss makes sure everyone knows right out of the gate he or she means business, we as parents need to do the same thing too. If a child isn't doing as directed, a favorite toy needs to be put on the shelf for the afternoon or an activity canceled. I am not a big fan of the timeout, because most children are pretty ambivalent about sitting on the step for five minutes. We need to take the time to find what small things will get a child's attention when they are deprived of them and use those things to drive behavior. This may sound slightly sinister, but it is no different than not touching a hot stove again after you've been burned. It is human nature and, as I've said, children are indeed human.

Use Encouragement and Rewards to Get the Behavior You Want: The bad boss never has anything nice to say, and you only get a raise because everyone gets a raise. The good boss, on the other hand, only has nice things to say and makes sure to tie a raise or bonus to something you did. For parents, once we have saying *No* and meaning what we say down, using encouragement and rewards will help you get the behavior you want. Encouragement is something that is both free and easy but, sadly, very rare. When you see your child do the tiniest thing the right way, you should be right there telling them that. In fact, we tend to do the opposite. We tell them when they've done something wrong or bad but fail to acknowledge the good. If we flip that around by encouraging the good and keeping quiet with the bad, we are accomplishing the same thing but in a much more positive manner. Since encouragement is a lot more enjoyable than silence, children will strive to do the things they know they need to do to get that pat on the back.

As for rewarding children, I've heard it said that we are actually bribing them, and this is incorrect.

A bribe is giving somebody something of value for doing something they are not supposed to do. A reward is giving someone something of value for doing something they are supposed to do. Also, people tend to immediately think of money when it comes to rewarding children. Giving allowances for doing household chores is certainly fine, but there is more value in rewarding children another way. Since we have become very good at saying and meaning *No*, now we can make our children work for *Yes*. The child will supply the opportunities because children are always asking for something. Therefore, once you have established that *No* means *No* but are willing to say *Yes*, every *Yes* should be *Yes, if*. Yes, *if* you clean the garage; yes, *if* you take your brother with you; yes, *if* you do the laundry. These are relatively simple examples, but the concept can be expanded to get some really big results. Previously I said that having a cell phone at school is a *No*, but under the right circumstances it could be a *Yes, if* the child brings home straight *A*s. This is a perfect example of using a reward to teach responsibility. The reason having a cell phone at school before the age of 16 was a *No* is it is unlikely the child will use it responsibly. School is a place to learn, not text your friends. However, once the ground rules are set, if the child proves they can act responsibility by getting and keeping good grades, then everyone is happy! This concept gets even bigger as children start to approach adulthood and decisions get harder. It isn't easy handing your 16-year-old the keys to the car on a Friday night, but if you've laid the foundation, your child will know that *Yes* is something to value and should not be taken lightly. If your child understands there are consequences to their actions and they need to work for the things they want, then you have done your job.

The last point on this rule is the first word of the rule: *Be* the boss. The things discussed here will not happen passively. Parents need to step up and take ownership of being the boss. Once you've taken ownership, you have to be relentless. Rest assured your children will be relentless and try to break you. They will do it in a nice way, but as we have said, life with a child is one long negotiation, and we have to stay frosty. Once these things are in place, the results can be very rewarding. Getting your children to act and behave the way you know they need to without screaming your head off is a very good thing.

RULE #8

Speak with One Voice

This is one that goes in the Surprise category for many parents. Parents can look at some of the rules we will go through and know, at least partially, that the rule is addressing a real problem. This one, however, isn't as obvious.

The issue is that one parent, whether consciously or not, will discount or disagree with the other parent in front of the child. Whether it is a disagreement about bedtime, punishment, something the child did, or something one of the parents thinks the child should do, parents have it out in front of the child.

You might be reading this and think, *so what? We shouldn't keep anything from our kids! We need to be open, and that includes arguments!* This seems like a pretty innocuous thing, but there are some serious consequences to playing out disagreements in front of the children.

A House Divided Against Itself Cannot Stand: This was true when Lincoln said it about the country, and it is true today when it comes to our own house. One of the themes that will run though this book is the need to establish a foundation that a child can always depend on; something that will always be unique to his or her family and, therefore, special. A cohesive parental team is one of those things that give children confidence and comfort. When Mom and Dad speak with one voice, the child knows what they are getting and have something they can depend on. The sum of the whole is much, much greater than the two parts. However, when a parental team splits into two individual parents, each doing it their own way, it forces the child to eventually take sides. The child may not want to take sides, but when confronted with two separate alternatives that is what has to happen.

Children Will Continually Push to Find Their Boundaries: Just like the rest of us, children will always be checking to see what they can get away with. Therefore, when they see a crack or a ray of light starting to separate their parents on anything, it is their natural response to try and drive a truck through it. It's like waking up in the morning and going to sleep at night. Have you ever sat with a child 7 or younger and not been shocked at the negotiating skills they have? Put a

6-year-old in charge of Middle East peace and it will probably get done in twenty minutes. They negotiate on everything because they are seeking out the end line:

If I eat three more bites can I have desert?

It's Sissy's turn to go first in the bathtub. I went first last time.

If you let me go to the party, I'll clean out the garage.

It takes willpower, guile, tenacity, and patience to fend off this constant onslaught. You want to give in and just say, "OK!" But you tough it out and stick to your guns.

However, if the other parent then walks in, gets the same pitch, and says, "Sure, that's fine!" they get the big hug, you get the look from the victorious child, and it's game over.

While we sort of know this to be true with older kids, we hold out hope that the little ones can't pick up on this yet, so it isn't critical that we get our stories straight while they are still in diapers. Unfortunately, this isn't the case. Toddlers and preschoolers view the world, including their parents, differently than older children do. They often see things in magical terms, as if simply asking for something is enough to make it appear. To children this age, parents are all-powerful (18). So, if I don't get what I want from parent *A*, why shouldn't

I ask parent *B*? They have the magic too! This is why they can look at you with those big doe eyes even when they know Mommy already said no. If you aren't on the same page with the other parent, those big doe eyes will run you ragged.

While the issue starts at an early age, the real problems occur when the child is older and knows what they are doing. If they are able to successfully play their parents off each other, then they are the one calling the shots, and no boundaries are set. As my wife often says, if parents don't set the boundaries for children, then they will set them on their own.

So, what do we do? There are a couple of easy guidelines to follow:

1) Keep a sharp eye: Sometimes the double-cross is easy to see coming, and sometimes the children are almost KGB-like in slipping you up. Any question that starts with "Can I" needs to be handled like kryptonite and subject to further review. There is nothing wrong with saying, "I'll think about it" and then going to talk it over with the other parent.

2) Never consciously cross up the other parent: I don't care if you walk in one day to find the other parent making the child stand on their head. Hold your tongue, tell the kid they probably deserve it, and then get ready to have it out with your counterpart when the

child is out of earshot. This is one of the hardest things for parents to do and something some just flat-out refuse to do. Again, since it isn't about you anymore, it is much more important to put up a united front to the child and then sort it out later.

Sometimes, however, if we can't work it out to a mutually agreeable course of action, someone just has to give in to the other parent's wishes in order to keep the front united. This is the lesser of the two evils because, in most cases, the difference between your opinion and the other parent's is minuscule compared to the ramifications of breaking up the parental team.

Giving in and accepting this is one of the sacrifices that come with being a good parent.

RULE #7

Own What Your Children Eat

It is impossible to overstate the issue of childhood nutrition and obesity. In the introduction, we went through the horrifying statistics: From 1980 to 2004 the prevalence of overweight children increased from 5.0 percent to 13.9 percent for children 2–5 years old, from 6.5 percent to 18.8 percent for children 6–11 years old, and from 5.0 percent to 17.4 percent for children 12–19 years old. Overweight children and adolescents are more likely to have risk factors associated with cardiovascular disease than are other children and adolescents. The incidents of Type 2 Diabetes among adolescents has increased by a factor of more than ten in the past two decades and may now exceed that of Type 1 Diabetes among black and Hispanic adolescents. New studies show millions of US children have disturbingly low Vitamin D levels, possibly increasing their risk for bone problems, heart disease, diabetes, and other ailments (19). The list goes on and on. The only good news in the last ten years is that the ever-increasing rates appear to have flattened out, but at an extremely alarming level

Our society, however, is in borderline denial over this. Parents are all too eager to point their fingers and not take ownership of the problem. Over the past few years we have seen McDonald's move into the role of evildoer when it comes to this. In 2002 McDonald's was sued for "failure to provide warnings about the dangers of eating fast food on frequent occasions and its failure to clearly showcase the amount of calories and fat in their menu items was a leading factor in causing a large amount of children to become obese and suffer harmful health problems due to their obesity" (20).

In the 2004 movie *Super Size Me*, the film follows what happens to the filmmaker's health while he eats all meals at McDonald's for thirty days straight. The results are not pretty. The filmmaker gains twenty pounds and gives his own physicians a health scare as they watch his health deteriorate.

All this has led, thankfully, to the fast-food industry increasing their offerings to include less destructive selections and putting some effort toward education on the subject of childhood nutrition. More is needed, and the marketing practices of the industry are rightly under scrutiny, but we have managed to overlook the point here that fast-food joints were never meant to be this country's dining room.

I am less surprised by the fact that fast food is unhealthy than I am by the fact that this seems to be a surprise to some people. It's fast food! It's greasy burgers and milkshakes! When I was a kid, fast food was a once-a-month treat. If my sister and I could catch Dad at a weak moment when Mom wasn't in the car, maybe we could squeeze two fast-food meals into a month. My parents knew that fast food is, in my mother's words, "processed crap." It's like candy. It tastes great, but it isn't good for you. This is something parents need to accept. It's not the fast-food industry's responsibility; it's our responsibility as parents.

We need to know and really own what our kids eat. We need to understand what it is they are eating and what it can do to them. Our children are becoming obese because almost everything they eat contributes to it. See how far off this menu is from what your child may eat on a daily basis:

Breakfast: Presweetened breakfast cereal, doughnut/ Danish, and juice.

Snack: Drinkable yogurt, snack bar, juice.

Lunch: Prepackaged lunch pack, microwave soup/dish/ meal, soda.

Snack: Cookies, crackers.

Dinner: Mac & cheese from a box, microwave dish/meal, fast food, soda.

Dessert: Ice cream bar.

Some of these things stand out as bad, but some sound just fine. Drinkable yogurt? Snack bar? Microwave soup? How can these be bad? The reason they are bad is because it is processed food. It's not the food itself as much as it is how it is made and with what.

The simple fact that everyone knows but doesn't want to admit is the human body was designed to work off of plants and the occasional poor little critter we could catch and eat. As we evolved and figured out how to work together, the animals we caught got bigger and grain was added as well, but the formula remained the same. This has been the way of the world since the beginning but changed drastically a short sixty years ago. The car, the drive-in, the supermarket, too busy to cook, a freezer in every kitchen, the microwave oven… this is when convenience made it a requirement that we add things to our food that the human body can't properly process and, in the end, pays the price for.

In his book, *The Blue Zone*, Dan Buettnen studies groups of people who have reached 100 years of age to find out why they made it a full century. During this search he finds four far-flung places on the earth where people are reaching age 100 at extraordinary rates or have a longer life expectancy. There are a few common factors, but when it comes to the food they eat, the two biggest factors are living off a plant-based diet and making it a point not to overeat. To put it in a nutshell, the things that help people live longer are in direct conflict with the fast-food super-sized meal of today.

So how do we break out of this trap? Here are six sub-rules to follow. There are only six, but make no mistake that living by them will be a drastic, yet necessary, change for you and your family.

Just One Fast-Food Meal per Week: That's still probably too much, but we have to start somewhere.

Introduce Veggies Into the Daily Diet: There's a reason why old people say, "Eat your vegetables!" It is what has to happen if you want your children to be healthy, and it has to happen every day.

No Processed Sugar at Breakfast: Fruits, grains, dairy, and some pure fruit juice instead.

Make Your Child's Lunch With Your Own Hands: A sandwich, celery or carrot sticks, and an apple or orange. If it's got a picture of something on it, then it doesn't go in the lunch.

Cut Out Soda and Processed Juices: Soda, like fast food, has gone from being a treat to replacing water in our children's diets. It needs to go back to being a treat. Just as bad these days are all juice and energy-drink products that are basically pure sugar. We need to get our children back to drinking water, milk, and pure juices. A food processor and a couple of pieces of fruit will do the trick.

If One of the First Three Ingredients in Something Is Corn Syrup, Cut It Out: Corn syrup today is made by changing the sugar in corn starch to fructose, and there is a good body of evidence out there saying that high levels of fructose lead to a higher percentage of health problems. There is some controversy about this, but the fact is that foods containing a significant amount of corn syrup are often high in calories and low in nutritional value, so therefore it's a good idea to just avoid them (21).

For a lot of people the changes outlined above are pretty significant, but they have to be made. First and foremost, this is not a negotiation. Don't ask the children if they will go along, just *be the boss* and make it so. The biggest ramification, however, is that someone is going to need to learn how to cook. It is common sense that people who know how to cook use the things we should be eating, and those who don't use what's convenient, which is made of things we shouldn't be eating. There is a reason why half our time spent on this earth up to sixty years ago was spent first acquiring and then preparing food. We have lost sight of this basic human function and are paying the price, or at least our children are. We need to see the light here immediately so our children don't forever lose the concept of eating correctly.

The upside here is that learning how to cook is a wonderful thing for the whole family to do and is a fun way to spend your time. It is rare that something that can save your life and the lives of your children is also fun to do, so dust off the big oven and get busy!

RULE #6

Reclaim Dinnertime

I was subjecting my family to a USC football game on TV one Saturday when I saw a commercial from Kentucky Fried Chicken telling us to restore family dinnertime by buying their product, taking it home, and having all family members sit together at the same time and consume it. My immediate thought was that it is a sad state of affairs when we need Kentucky Fried Chicken to remind us that the family dinner is important. In this fast-paced, soccer-practice, someone-has-to-work-late world, why is having dinner together every night important? There are some facts, and then there are the reasons behind the facts. Let's start with the facts:

1) More mealtime at home was shown in a 1999 University of Michigan study to be the single strongest predictor of better achievement scores and fewer

behavioral problems in children. Mealtime was more powerful than time spent in school, studying, church, playing sports, or art activities (22). A 1994 Lou Harris *Reader's Digest* national poll of high school seniors showed higher scholastic scores among students who frequently shared meals with their families. Also, a survey of high-achieving teens showed that those who regularly eat meals with their families tend to be happier with their present life and their prospects for the future (23).

2) A federally funded study of American teenagers found a strong association between regular family meals (five or more dinners per week with a parent) and academic success; psychological adjustment; and lower rates of alcohol use, drug use, early sexual behavior, and suicide risk (24).

3) A medical study of children ages 9–14 found that those who have more regular dinners with their families have more healthful dietary patterns, including more fruits and vegetables, less saturated and trans fat, fewer fried foods and sodas, and more vitamins and other micronutrients (25). A Harvard study showed that eating family dinners together most or all days of the week was associated with eating more healthfully. The study showed that families eating meals together "every day" or "almost every day" generally consumed higher amounts of important nutrients such as calcium; fiber; Vitamins B6, B12, C, and E; and iron and that they

consumed less overall fat compared to families who "never" or "only sometimes" ate meals together (26).

4) A National Center for Substance Abuse study found that the more often children share the evening meal with their families, the less likely they are to smoke, drink, or use drugs. Teens that have two or less family dinners per week compared to teens that have five family dinners are three times more likely to try marijuana, two and a half times more likely to smoke cigarettes, and more than one and a half times more likely to drink alcohol (27).

This is a pretty impressive list. Children do better in school, are less likely to get into trouble, and eat healthier. Those are three results most parents would be pretty happy with. The question, though, is why? There are many reasons that, surprisingly, touch multiple aspects of our lives and how we learn.

The Daily Family Meal Provides Children With a "Safe Harbor": As we all know deep down in our hearts, being a child can be very tough. Children can, for lack of a better term, be ruthless with one another. Children will say things to each other that are downright cruel. School is no picnic, either. Life can get to be pretty overwhelming for a child. That is why it is so vitally important that they have a place they can go every day—a safe harbor—where they are part of the clan and given positive attention. It's like Norm walking into the bar on *Cheers*.

Children Need a Forum: There are a lot of things running around in a child's head that need to be expressed. These can be concerns, questions, or ideas. It's important that children have a regular opportunity to express themselves in a comfortable forum.

The Communal Aspect of the Family Dinner Is Very Important: The family tradition of parents providing for the children and all sharing what the family collectively has is a large part of what the family dinner is. It's important for children to experience having food passed to them and, conversely, passing food to someone else.

The Family Dinner Gives Children a Positive Regimen: We as adults understand what it feels like to have the world spinning out of control, and children feel the same way. The family dinner provides children with a regimen that helps provide the comfort that comes with structure in our daily lives. The family dinner is a daily event where everyone can reboot and get ready for the next day.

Children Need to Learn Healthy Eating: We have covered this area in detail, but the best place to learn this is sitting at the dinner table and not getting any dessert until you finish your broccoli.

Families Need Bonding Time: This is no surprise, but it is surprising how little time families actually spend together today, and text-messaging doesn't count. The family dinner table is where we tell stories of what happened when Mom and Dad were kids and that time Grandma fell in the lake. Being in a family means having a special connection, but that connection doesn't just happen. It has to be worked on.

Parents Need to Monitor Their Children: *Monitoring* is a buzzword in business meaning you know what is happening when it is happening. If we don't take time daily to ask questions and observe our children's mood and behavior, we are quickly going to be out of touch. Who are their friends? What are they doing after school? How are they doing in math? Are they upset at anyone? These are things we need to keep on top of, and the family dinner is the best mechanism for doing so.

Children Need to Learn the Art of Conversation: Eventually children will grow up and need to communicate with other adults. They will need to know how to use language and engage in conversation. The family dinner gives them the opportunity to observe adult conversation and engage in it.

Children Need to Learn Table Manners: Along the same lines, children will grow up and, at some time, be required to eat with other people. I never had a high opinion of my own table manners until I saw what the youth of today are bringing to the table. This is something that children today need lots of practice at.

It will take effort on everyone's part to make family dinner happen, and it won't happen every single night. Four out of seven nights a week is a good target for families who are currently family dinner–challenged. As we discussed in "Own What Your Children Eat," instituting the family dinner requires that someone is going to have to learn how to cook. Fortunately, there are a great number of resources now for learning how to prepare quick, healthy, and good-tasting food every day without a lot of trouble. The benefits, as we've seen, far outweigh the trouble.

RULE #5

Turn Whatever Is On Off, and Go Outside

This rule is something still ringing in my own ears from childhood. I am part of the first TV generation of the 1960s and can still hear my mother saying, "Turn that G.D. TV off and go outside!" Today, though, it isn't just the TV; it's Wii, iPhones, Twitter, YouTube, and Facebook as well. Regardless, my mother's words are just as valid and true today. We need to stop fostering a society of shut-ins who never look up and get our children to play outside like the countless generations before them. This rule packs a double punch because it starts with getting your children to stop doing something they shouldn't do so much and start doing something they should do more of.

First off, I am not anti-TV. Truth be told, my children watch some TV almost every day. This TV-watching includes *Tom and Jerry*, which has lots of head-bashing.

I do not scorn television or look down on anyone who watches it or lets their children watch it. Same thing with the computer. That being said, we all know watching too much TV and spending too much time on the computer and constantly pounding away at that little electronic device in your hands is bad for you. If anyone says differently, they are not being honest with themselves. If people need proof, there is plenty of it (28):

Academic achievement drops sharply for children who watch more than ten hours a week of TV, according to a report from the U.S. Department of Education.

The same report stated that three factors—student absenteeism, no variety of reading material in the home, and excessive TV-watching—account for nearly 90 percent of the difference in the average performance of eighth-graders' mathematics scores.

As far back as 1994 (before the Internet boom), American children spent more time watching TV than they did in school.

Sixth- and twelfth-grade California students who were heavy viewers of TV scored lower on reading, written expression, and math achievement tests than students who viewed little or no television.

A 2004 study showed that early TV viewing (ages 1 and 3 were studied) is associated with attention problems (ADHD) at a later age (age 7).

Video games have the same issues and more if there is some sort of violence involved. While watching violent acts on TV is exposure violence, playing video games is like practicing the same violent acts over and over again, with rewards for improvement. It is common sense to realize that children will become desensitized to violence if they simulate it every day. On top of this, interactive sites like Twitter and Facebook allow us to basically now be on TV starring in our own soap operas.

As you might imagine, with the explosion of video games and the Internet over the past fifteen years, the amount of time children spend in front of some screen has increased dramatically. The average amount of time children ages 8 to 18 spent watching TV every day in 2004 was the same as in 1999, at three hours and five minutes. Video games and computer use, however, has increased from fifty-three minutes a day to an hour and fifty-one minutes per day (29). I thought I watched a lot of TV when I was a kid, but the only time I watched more than three hours a day was when I was home sick. However, today children are spending an average of five hours a day in front of some sort of screen. It's time to turn whatever it is that is on, off.

Now we need to go outside. I'm not talking about the weekly tee ball/soccer practice or play date with at least two parents watching over everything, but about good old-fashioned go-outside-and-play. A recent University of San Diego study showed that children age 9 spend an average of three hours a day outside, but by age 15 that is down to 45 minutes a day and only 35 minutes a day on weekends (30). These trends are going the wrong way. Children need to be outside for both the body and spirit. Here is a list of benefits of outdoor activity, as compiled by the US Fish and Wildlife Service (31):

- Children who interact with nature have better cognitive and creative skills than their housebound counterparts.

- Interaction with the environment can help children reduce stress.

- Children who interact regularly with nature show improved test scores.

So why does playing outside provide these benefits? Simply put, playing outside lets a kid be a kid.

Imagination Training: For children to learn and develop, they have to put their imagination to work. This is how they become creative thinkers and problem-solvers. There is no better place to practice imagination then in the backyard with a pile of dirt, some sticks, and some rocks. This is also something that can't be forced, as in "Go imagine something!" We need to put children in an environment where imagination will come out of necessity.

Freedom to Get Dirty: We worry a lot about stress relief, blowing off steam, etc. This is an issue for our kids as well. Nothing is a better stress-reliever, however, than to go muck it up outside, and usually the widest grins are on the dirtiest kids.

Independence Training: When we are constantly looking over our children's shoulders, it's impossible for them to develop the independent streak they will desperately need to succeed when they are adults. Giving them time on their own makes them comfortable with being alone and doing things on their own.

Quality Family Time: While we should let our children spend a good deal of time outside without us hovering, doing activities outside together is an excellent opportunity to build up that elusive quality time we are always looking for. Taking time to go to the park, throw a ball around, fly a kite, take a walk, or hunt for lizards is the best way to get close and stay close to your children. Unfortunately, in too many instances today a child going outside requires an adult going with them, so quality family time becomes a bonus to just getting the children outside regularly.

Health: Besides the issues we've covered regarding diet, our children lack exercise. Being a kid outside is an anaerobic activity and needs to be encouraged. Again, playing on a soccer team is great, but it's the little strides made by being active outside every day that will make the difference for children with weight and health issues.

As the American Academy of Pediatrics' Dr. Kenneth Ginsburg testified to Congress in 2006, "Play allows children to create and explore a world they can master, conquering their fears while practicing adult roles.... Play helps children develop new competencies...and the resiliency they will need to face future challenges."

Certainly this is not as easy as it was for past generations, where kids were told to go out and just be home before the streetlights went on. Sadly, this is a different world, and safety is a major concern for everyone. Also, the necessity for both parents to work or the pressure of running a single-parent family doesn't make things any easier. This is something, though, that as parents we need to be conscious of and not let any opportunity to get outside pass us by. We need to recognize when our children have been staring at that screen for more than two hours and break the trance. We need to have alternatives at the ready. If that is sending them out into the backyard, fantastic. If there is no backyard, then it's going to require a little more work and effort, but those children have to get outside.

RULE #4

Require Respect and Manners

The title of this chapter was originally "Demand Respect and Manners," but I was concerned that title conveyed the idea that our children owe us and society respect and manners. Some might believe that is the case, but I don't, and I think that notion is counterproductive. Our children are not obligated to behave a certain way, nor do they owe society anything that can be "paid off" by showing good manners and respect. Thinking this way is likely to provoke some feeling of resentment toward society, which doesn't get us anywhere.

Society doesn't demand respect and manners, but it does require it for a child to have the best chance of being accepted and successful. Why is this? Because when we meet someone for the first time we have to have a commonly understood code of conduct to gauge whether this new person is someone we should like, embrace, or be wary of. When we meet people for the first time who are polite and show respect, we are inclined to do the same. Therefore, showing respect and being polite means that more times than not, society will be very welcoming to you. This makes life a lot easier. However, when we meet someone who is cold, snappy, or downright rude, we are more inclined to act that way right back. Interacting with a hostile society can be a very difficult, frustrating, and embittering experience. I once had someone who worked for me ask if we could talk in private. Once the door was closed, he asked me why I was so formal with him while I was a lot more open and relaxed with his peers. This is a person who never smiled; gave short, curt answers to every question; and never took his hat off. I explained that his behavior toward me dictated my behavior toward him. If you want respect and to be treated with kindness, you have to first be willing to do it yourself.

This is the reason we need to require respect and manners from our children. When it comes time for them to set out and meet society for the first time, society will judge them and, therefore, engage them based on how our children engage society. It is unreasonable to expect society to embrace a child who acts like they don't want to be embraced. On the other hand, the vast majority of people will open up like a flower on a warm spring day when they encounter a child who says "Excuse me," "Please," and "Thank you." This is something you can observe every day by simply looking for it. When you see a child display good manners and show respect, observe how they are treated. Also, when you see a child not look someone in the eye, mumble something, and then walk away without saying thank you, take note of how that child was perceived and take a guess at how he or she will be treated in the future by that person.

As you can see, this is a vicious cycle, and that is why we, as parents, need to make certain our children don't get caught in it. If children are rude, they are likely to be treated rudely. If they are treated rudely, they are likely to be resentful and act more rudely, etc. This is critical because acting rudely is not simply an undesirable trait. It has some significant ramifications. First, the vicious cycle described above can severely affect a child's view of the world and cause a great deal of anger and anxiety. It is hard to get ahead when every day is a slog and you think the world is out to get you. Next, rude behavior will limit job and advancement opportunities. Again, would-be employers are put off by rude behavior and can usually find someone just as capable who won't behave like an ass. The TV drama *House* is very popular because it gives comfort to those who think their skill and contribution to society should trump their boorish behavior. The show is about Dr. Gregory House, who is such a gifted diagnostician that his ability to figure out why people are sick keeps him employed even though he is one of the rudest people on the planet. *House* is popular because it would be easier if that's how life was.

As long as we can display our genius to save the world, who cares if we act like a brat? We all do need to realize, though, that it is a TV show, because if it were the real world, Dr. House would be fired halfway through every episode. There are also life-threatening aspects to rude behavior that shouldn't be ignored. According to the National Highway Traffic Safety Administration, aggressive drivers (drivers who tailgate, exceed speed limits, run red lights, and switch lanes with no warning) contribute to the more than 6 million crashes in the US each year. It may sound trivial on the surface, but the fact is, manners are important for a child when it comes to job opportunities, social opportunities, safety, and happiness.

Requiring respect and manners is, like most of the other rules in the book, something that requires a good deal of effort on the part of parents. It isn't a matter of telling your children to show respect and manners; you have to teach them, and that takes some time. The key is to be relentless and consistent. Here are points of emphasis to concentrate on:

When They Want Something Require "Please" in a Complete Sentence: This is something you will end up doing about four to six times a day. Children will always ask for things, and it usually comes out as, "I want some milk." You then say, "How do you ask properly?" and the child says, "Please." Since this is reactive and not proactive, you need to go back and have them start again: "May I please have some milk?" After six or seven years, they start to get the hang of it.

Over-Require "Excuse Me" and "Thank You": Some would say that you can't say "Excuse me" and "Thank you" enough, and that's what we need to teach our children. If you pick up the crayon they dropped on the floor and hand it to them, they should say "Thank you." When the person behind the counter gives them back their change, they should say "Thank you." "Thank you" needs to become a reflex.

Require Your Children to Look People in the Eye When Speaking or Being Spoken to: This is something that is tough for a small child, but it doesn't get any easier unless you get used to doing it.

Have Your Children Order Their Own Food at Restaurants and Ask for Things Themselves: I've seen some parents still ordering for their teenage children. Eating out is the perfect opportunity for children to practice their manners on someone they don't know. Practice makes perfect.

Your Children Should Address All Adults Formally Until Given Permission Not to: It doesn't have to be as formal as Mr. Smith or Mrs. Jones. Mr. John or Miss Cheryl is perfectly fine. In a lot of cases, the adult will insist that your child only use their given name, and that's great. No adult lights up more than when saying, "Now, you can call me Allen!" You only get here, however, if you start with respect.

Require Your Male Children to Take Their Hats Off When Appropriate: Over the last twenty years, the cap seems to have become part of a young male's anatomy, since they never come off. It is a sign of disrespect, however, when the lid stays on in a restaurant or someone's home. If our young men are so worried about society showing them respect, this is a good place for them to start.

Require Your Children to Open Doors for Other People: Very important for the male children but also important for the females, as well. Again, you will never see an adult's face light up faster than when a child opens a door for them.

It's important to emphasize that in their lives, our children will encounter many foul and bitter people. Regardless of how our children behave toward these people, they will be mean and nasty. This is the way of the world. The best way to root out the truly mean and nasty is to display respect and manners. If you give a person no excuse for treating you rudely and they still do, you know who that person really is. Our problem is, our children don't put their best foot forward and think the worst of the world when it doesn't jump out with arms opened wide. Since the truly mean and nasty are a minority, our children need to let everyone else know that they can participate and thrive in a civil society, and that requires respect and manners.

RULE #3

Show Up

About two years ago I had an epiphany that led, in large part, to writing this book. As I was leaving for work, my wife said, "Sorry I forgot to tell you, but our daughter's pre-K Spring Celebration is today at 1:00 pm." What, I asked, was the Spring Celebration? Basically, the four-year-old class would sing about four songs, and then everyone would have cookies. My wife apologized for not telling me sooner and understood if I couldn't make it. My schedule was pretty packed, so I left the house with the thought that I would skip the event. Fortunately, a two-hour meeting got canceled at the last minute, so I was able to jump in the car and race over to the preschool. Huffing and puffing, I plopped down into an open seat with about fifteen seconds to spare.

I watched the kids march in, and my daughter was fourth from the last in line. She scanned the audience, and when she saw me she became a completely different person. She broke out into a grin she tried to suppress but couldn't and immediately walked a little taller and bouncier. She sang the four songs with great enthusiasm and gave me a big hug at the end with that grin still beaming. My showing up made a huge difference.

However, my daughter's experience was not where the epiphany came from. It came from the child immediately behind my daughter in line when the children walked in. Just like my daughter scanned the crowd, so did this little girl. Where my daughter's face lit up when she saw me, this little girl's face became ashen when she realized her parents weren't there. While my daughter stood tall and sang like a bird, this little girl stood slumped, just waiting for the thing to be over. Her mother did fortunately arrive in time to hear the last song, and she brightened a bit. I will never, however, forget the contrast between the two and what it means to a child to see their parents at this type of thing.

Therefore, Rule #3 is "Show Up." Being there means far more to your children than you realize and, consequently, not being there hurts far more than you realize. What this boils down to is if you are there for the Spring Celebrations and the soccer games and the dance recitals and the bike parades, it demonstrates to your children exactly how important they are to you.

They know adults have lots of things going on and have to do grown-up stuff, so to put that aside and show them that they are the most important thing to you simply by showing up is hugely important. On the other hand, if you don't show up, the message is exactly the opposite. If there is something more important for you to do than be there at these things, then the child knows there is something more important than them, plain and simple. You may be off the hook if no parents show up, but that seldom happens.

When it comes to school, there is a mound of evidence that shows when parents show up and participate at their child's school the child's academic performance improves dramatically. Family participation in education is twice as predictive of a student's academic success as family socioeconomic status (32). The more parents participate in schooling in a sustained way at every level—in advocacy, decision-making and oversight roles, as fund-raisers and boosters, as volunteers and paraprofessionals, and as home teachers—the better for student achievement (33). When remembering his first back-to-school night as a student teacher, Robert Freeman felt uneasy. When his master teacher asked why, he said, "All the wrong parents came." He then explained that the parents of the "good" students came, when he had hoped to see the parents of the students who never turned in their homework, were always late to class, etc. His colleague then said, "That's why your good students are good students" (34).

Showing up sounds easy enough, but the reason most parents aren't there every time they should be is that it can be difficult. We need to juggle a lot of things to make this happen. Here are some guidelines to follow in making this rule a reality:

Identify Attendance-Mandatory Events Well in Advance: This should be done at the beginning of every school year, at the midyear point, and at the start of any extracurricular activity. A master family schedule should be kept where everyone can see it so there are no surprises. The events that are attendance-mandatory are:

- **Any Performance:** School play, class concert, dance recital, band performance, etc.

- **Any Game:** Soccer, T-ball, softball, baseball, volleyball, basketball, football, etc.

- **Any Parent-Teacher Conference or School Open House**

Remember Rule #10: It's not about you anymore, so if there is a conflict you need to move heaven and earth to make it work. If one of these events interferes with something you like to do personally, you need put the attendance-mandatory event first on your list.

Be On Time: If you end up being fifteen minutes late all the time, don't bother going. No child wants to be the kid with the parent who's always late.

Volunteer to Coach a Team or Lead an Activity: There are never enough parents to do the work required to run a soccer team or a Brownie troop, so step up and volunteer. Not only will you be showing your child how important they are, you will be helping a lot of other children as well.

Volunteer at Your Child's School: Again, there are never enough parents to fill the need, and the need grows greater every year. The reasons are the same as volunteering to coach or lead an activity, with the added bonus that you get to observe how your child is doing in class. To state the obvious, the time our children spend in school is incredibly important, and while we can talk to our child's teacher and see the report card, an opportunity to actually observe your child in the classroom shouldn't be passed up.

Let me add one more thing when it comes to parent-teacher conferences and volunteering at school. There seems to be a growing sense that teachers are ultimately responsible for how our children turn out, particularly from an academic standpoint. Raising our children is not a teacher's responsibility; it's a parent's responsibility. The teacher's responsibility is to present important and very useful information to our children, which the vast majority does with skill and dedication. It is the parent's responsibility to make sure our child is ready, willing, and able to take that information and do something with it. In order to do that effectively, we must establish a good, solid working relationship with our children's teachers. We should treat them like family when it comes to knowing how our children are doing. No one has greater insight into what might be troubling a child than the teacher who sees them day in and day out as they learn and interact with other kids. Teachers need our support to be successful teachers, and we need their input to be successful parents. We also have to keep in mind that while we have a limited number of children, teachers have an ever-growing number of students, so we need to do the lion's share of the work.

Simply put, you have to be there. You have to be there at important events in your child's life. Remember, there are only about fifteen years of actual childhood. Once children turn sixteen, the childhood clock is winding down. Childhood is actually a short period of time, and you can't get it back. You need to be there, you need to be seen, and you need to see what's going on in your child's life. No one will care twenty years later that you sat on that conference call for an hour and a half instead of attending your child's school bazaar. If you don't know what a school bazaar is, don't worry about it. Just show up.

RULE #2

Read with Your Kids

It probably isn't a surprise that this rule made the list, but some might wonder why it comes in at number two. It's number two because it's that important.

As discussed in the introduction, and as every parent feels in their heart, our children are falling behind the rest of the world when it comes to academic achievement. This has serious ramifications for our children's future as well as our society's future. There are long lists of why this is, and an even longer list of what we can do about it, but the place we need to start is to get our children to fall in love with reading again. Reading needs to be something children want to do, not something they think they have to do. It needs to be something they look forward to, not a chore. This is another one of those things that has changed greatly over the last twenty to thirty years. According to the 2008 Kids and Family Reading Report by children's book publisher Scholastic, children today are reading less and less for fun. Only one in four kids reads for fun daily. In the 2006 report, three out of ten kids read for fun each day; 22 percent of kids rarely, if ever, read for fun; and half of all kids think there just aren't any interesting books for them (35).

The reason this is critical is because reading is the gateway to learning. If you don't read well, you won't learn well. If you don't like reading, you won't like learning. This may sound a little harsh, but there are only two ways humans can absorb a large amount of information: by hearing someone talk or by reading. If we expect our children to compete with the rest of the world simply based on what they hear from the teacher in the classroom, then we are going to be greatly disappointed. That isn't going to happen because, even if we have the best teachers, 100-percent-attentive children, and maximize the amount of actual teaching time in our schools, there simply isn't enough time for children to learn everything they need to know. At some point children are going to need to do most of the heavy lifting of learning themselves, and for that they will need to not only be able to read but like it. If they don't like to read, then learning most likely isn't going to happen. Children need to be comfortable with reading and enjoy it so they can access the information they need to be successful in life. This is something that was well understood until the media-technology revolution that started with the television began to chip away at this simple fact of life.

As a child, I remember the house being full of books and my parents regularly reading for fun. Rest assured we were not a bookish lot, either. We were the norm more than the exception. I remember spending hours just looking through books even before I knew how to read, because I saw my parents reading. When I did learn to read, I loved getting a new book from the school library and taking it home. Later, my friend and I could kill a whole afternoon at the public library. Again, we were not exceptional (to which my mediocre grades would attest) but normal, everyday kids. Most of the kids I knew in junior high school and high school read for fun. *Lord of the Rings* made for three great movies, but reading those books as a teen was ten times as fun and trained a generation to not blink at a thick book.

We have to get our children comfortable with reading and help them to enjoy it. The best way to do this is to read with them. You can either read to them or have them read to you. This is not a new concept.

"Children are made readers on the laps of their parents."

—Emilie Buchwald

"There are many little ways to enlarge your child's world. Love of books is the best of all."

—Jacqueline Kennedy

"The more you read, the more things you will know. The more that you learn, the more places you'll go."

—Dr. Seuss

"The greatest gift is a passion for reading."

—Elizabeth Hardwick

"The non-reading children are the greatest problem in American education."

—Glenn Doman,

"Once you learn to read, you will be forever free."

—Frederick Douglass

And there have also been studies done that prove this point. A National Reading Panel study found that there is ample evidence that one of the major differences between poor and good readers is the difference in the quantity of total time they spend reading. The study also concluded that students who do not develop reading fluency, regardless of how bright they are, are likely to remain poor readers throughout their lives (36).

So, how do we change our family culture in regard to reading? Here is a list of steps to take:

Read with Your Children for Fifteen Minutes Every Day: Like every other skill, reading takes practice, and the best way to practice anything is to do a little bit each day. Reading should be an every-day event, just like eating. Right before bed is a perfect time to make and keep your "reading date." For younger children, read aloud to them and don't worry if they want to hear the same story over and over. This will help them become familiar with words and, therefore, will make it easier to learn how to read the words when that time comes. For older children, have them read to you. You can trade off with the child reading some shorter books or stories and you reading longer stories.

Make Books Part of Life: Give them as gifts to your children and each other. Put up bookshelves and make books just as much a part of the house as the TV and family pictures.

Carve Out Family Reading Time: If you have children who are now, sadly, too old to read with you at bedtime, then carve out some family time where everyone reads independently. This is a good way to set an example and demonstrate that reading is a lifelong endeavor. Who knows, you might even read a few books you like!

Make Reading a Game: When you are out and about, quiz your children on signs you see. You can also have reading contests at home. Everyone make a stack of books at the beginning of summer, and the first one to finish the stack wins.

Introduce Your Children to the Newspaper: In my family, the one thing that was read by everyone every day was the *Los Angeles Times*. Whether it was the front page, sports section, Metro, or Calendar section, everyone read some portion of that paper every day for entertainment and information. Newspapers educate, inform, and make children better readers. Sadly, newspapers are struggling and not what they once were, but even as a collection of AP wire stories, they can help children fall in love with reading. If you are currently getting the paper, walk your older children through it so they know where to go to find the things they like. If you aren't getting a paper, start getting one. It will make a big difference, and Lord knows the newspaper industry needs all the subscribers it can get.

Your child won't be successful unless they not only know how to read but are good at it. The only way they will become good at it is if they like it. The only way they will end up liking reading is if you, as the parent, make it part of the family's life. The nice thing about reading is, once you get them started, the wonder of a good story will take it from there.

RULE #1

Do the Right Thing

This is rule number one because if you forget all the others but live this one day in and day out, you'll be just fine. The day-in-and-day-out aspect is crucial because, as a parent, you will be confronted daily with situations and decisions that will beg the question, "What is the right thing to do?"

This daily exercise is what makes this rule so important. The two things that make it difficult are:

1) Knowing what the right thing is..
2) Doing it.

When it comes to knowing, most parents have a good feel for what the right thing is, but there are so many outside influences, it's hard to see it clearly day to day and stay consistent.

The best way to know what the right thing to do is day to day and to be consistent is to define what a parent's responsibilities are. The three responsibilities parents should accept for themselves and live by when it comes to their children are:

Protector of Body and Soul: This sounds like a no-brainer, but sometimes we all need reminding on the *body* part and, frankly, we need to beef up our efforts on the *soul* part. When it comes to our children's physical well-being, we parents today can be accused of going through the motions when the children are young and giving in a little as our children get older. Let's take the car, for example. For younger children, we have the car seat and booster seat, but is it actually installed properly? Since children grow quickly, are the straps positioned correctly? Did you move your child out of the booster seat too soon because it was more convenient? When you drive with your children, do you give your full attention to what's happening on the road? Studies show that over 100,000 children under the age of 10 are injured in car accidents every year and less than 20 percent of the children between the ages of 4 and 8 are properly restrained (37).

For older children who are chomping at the bit to either get behind the wheel or jump in the car with their friends, it is very hard to say no. However, motor vehicle crashes are the leading cause of death for US teens, accounting for more than one in three deaths in this age group. In 2005, twelve teens ages 16 to 19 died every day from motor vehicle injuries, and nearly 400,000 motor vehicle occupants in this age group sustained nonfatal injuries that required treatment in an emergency department (38). The car is the biggest example, but it is just one. As parents we need to do the right thing when it comes to our children's physical safety and walk the walk as well as talk the talk.

Protecting the soul is equally important and becomes more challenging by the day. "Lost innocence" is an overused term, but the thing to remember about lost innocence when we are talking about our children is that it can't be recovered. Once it is lost, it is gone. If we are to stay true to our role as protectors, then we need to do everything in our power to make sure our children stay as innocent as possible for as long as possible. We do this by knowing everything there is to know about our children's lives. Who are their friends? What are they reading? What are they watching? Where are they going? What are they listening to? What are they doing on the computer? Some will say this is an invasion of privacy but, trust me, I've looked it up, and there are no laws against being a nosy parent. Once we know these things, we can make decisions about what and who are right and appropriate for our child. Again, there will be some unhappy children when you act in your role as protector, but you're not trying to win a popularity contest, you are trying to protect your child, and it is thus perfectly fine to err on the side of caution.

Life Trainer: As anyone over the age of 25 knows, life gets pretty complicated and pretty difficult pretty fast. Once our children reach adulthood they are going to have to make a lot of difficult choices on their own. When we use the term "trainer," think of the Burgess Meredith character in the *Rocky* movies. We have eighteen years to prepare our children to join society as contributing members standing on their own two feet. To do so, there needs to be a lot of teaching, a lot of hand-holding, some cajoling, some discipline, and, above all, a lot of encouragement. The goal is not to make the child happy now but to prepare them to be as independent and successful as possible when the time comes for them to do things on their own. When you ask yourself if you're doing the right thing, you need to think about what is best for preparing your child to stand on their own two feet.

Role Model: Back at the height of his playing career, the basketball player Charles Barkley made a controversial TV commercial where he emphatically stated that he, as a basketball player, was not a role model but that parents are role models. Sir Charles, as he is known, came under a lot of criticism for this, but, in fact, he was exactly right. The best, and some would say only, place a child is going to learn how to act is at home. You have to remember that a child can't compare and contrast behavior being exhibited by his or her parent with another adult. There isn't the aptitude or the opportunity to do that at an early age. What a child sees a parent do is what they will emulate, so make it count. At the 2008 Summer Olympics, swimmer Michael Phelps won an astonishing eight gold medals. Phelps is a phenomenal physical talent, but to accomplish what he did required more than talent. It required a work ethic, perseverance, and the respect of his teammates to make it all happen. Where did he learn this? From Mom, of course. At a joint interview the night after Phelps had won the last of his eight gold medals, Bob Costas asked Debbie Phelps if she could actually go back and do her job as a middle school principal considering all the attention. Before she could answer, Michael, with a great deal of pride in his voice, said, "I can answer that...she will." Michael went on to say how hard-working and dedicated his mom was and that he and his sisters could see that as kids. He said as children you try to model yourself after what your parents do and how well they do it. Since that time Michael Phelps has made some bad choices, paid a price, and no doubt really agitated his mother. It is a rule of nature that it isn't a matter of if a person growing up will make a mistake but when, and it's the same for everyone. The key is what you do after the mistake and, again, having a role model to be a guide is critical. Mr. Phelps would be well served to emulate the standard set by his mother in the future.

Now that we have established the role in which parents should decide and act, we come to the hardest part: actually doing the right thing. It is sometimes a lot easier to know what the right thing to do is than to actually do it. There is usually the easy thing to do and the right thing to do. The easy path calls to us because it's usually the popular choice as well. Confronted by these choices day in and day out, the easy choice begins to feel like a warm bath. Everyone will cheer, and you get to move on. The right thing to do, however, often will feel like a cold shower. Taking that path day in and day out takes courage, determination, and discipline. The easiest way to summon those strengths when you need them is to keep your eye on the prize, as they say. We aren't placing individual bricks but building a wall. The quality and character of that wall will be determined by how carefully and properly we place each individual brick. Placing those brinks correctly calls upon us to do the right thing on a daily basis when it comes to our children.

CONCLUSION

So there you have it: *Ten Simple Rules for Being a Better Parent in a World Turned Upside Down.* One of the things I hear a lot when getting feedback from parents is they expected it to be *Ten Easy Rules for Being a Better Parent,* but *Simple* and *Easy* aren't the same thing. The cold, hard fact is that being a good parent is not at all easy. It is hard. It is hard to do, and it takes a lot of work. I go back to the analogy we used in the last rule about building a wall brick by brick. We are not only building a wall, we are building the Great Wall of China. It is very hard to build a 4,000-mile-long wall over mountain ranges, and it is certainly a lot of work. If you commit to it, though, and do it right, you will have helped create something the world will be better off having and, in the end, that is what every parent's goal should be: delivering to society a person who will contribute to making the world a better place. Some don't agree with this. There has been a choir of voices, like author Ayelet Waldman, saying, "Yeah, I'm a bad

mother, so what? What we are doing is good enough"
(39). True, we can certainly get too wound up about
being perfect parents, and sometimes good enough is
just that, but shouldn't we give our absolute best effort
to the one true product of our time on earth?

The other major theme of the feedback I get is what
I left out. There is a long list of issues facing parents
today that are not specifically addressed:

Should the two parents marry?

If they are married, do they stay married no matter
what?

Should the mother work or stay at home?

Is it all right to spank your child?

At what age should a child be allowed to date?

How do you deal with your child wanting to drink,
smoke, or do drugs?

How do you talk about sex?

If I had tried to tackle all the dilemmas facing parents
today, it would have been a lot more rules than ten, so
I boiled it down to the ten chosen because they cover
critical factors that affect all aspects of a child's life.

For the questions I listed above and any others I left out, let's call them Bookend Questions. They are Bookend Questions because if you apply Rule #10 and Rule #1 you will get the answer you are looking for. For all of these unanswered questions, if you remind yourself that it's not about you anymore and ask yourself what is the right thing to do, then you will be just fine. If you married early in life and have children but are finding your marriage to not be what you hoped, remind yourself that it's not about you anymore, and ask yourself what the right thing to do is. If your young child just keeps pushing your buttons at the wrong place and time, remind yourself that it's not about you anymore, and ask yourself what the right thing to do is. I have not provided answers to these two questions because the answer could be different from person to person.

The ten simple rules are the ten simple rules because they pretty much apply at all times to everyone. There really isn't a time where it's bad to show up at one of your child's events, as an example. The more difficult questions need to be answered on a case-by-case basis, but as long as you remind yourself that it's not about you anymore and ask yourself what the right thing to do is, you should be fine.

As we end, we have to talk about why we should do all this. Why would I want to build The Great Wall of

China when I can just take them to the drive-through and plop them down in front of the TV every day?

First, our society will not survive unless parents do a better job, because the job of parenting has to be done. A good example of this is the work done by a nonprofit in Seaside, CA, called Community Partnership for Youth (CPY). Seaside was a military town until 1993 when Fort Ord closed. Through the 1990s Seaside suffered through gang and crime issues. CPY was founded by people in the community looking to intervene and help the city's kids get on track. CPY has achieved great results helping at-risk youths by teaching the children in the program six standards (40):

- In CPY, we greet each other every day with a smile and handshake to strengthen the relationship between us.
- In CPY, we honor and respect each other so we address one another with the proper language and speech.
- In CPY, we value the space of ourselves and others and are careful not to intrude or injure each other.
- In CPY, we are mindful of what is true and strive to be honest in word and deed.
- In CPY, we treasure our rich heritage and hold the cultures of all people in high regard.
- In CPY, we strive to reflect our beauty both inwardly in our understanding and outwardly in our appearance.

These standards are basic parenting. If every parent imparted these standards to their children, the world would be a better place. This is a clear example that children don't do well without parenting, so parenting is required if we want our children to succeed. Organizations like CPY are great, and we need to support and promote them, but there are only so many CPYs out there, and the money to fund these initiatives has gotten very scarce. If we think that these institutions will do the job of preparing our children to succeed, we are going to be disappointed. Parents have to do the job.

Second, and on a more personal note, parents who have successful and happy children are a lot happier than parents who don't. If you have an unhappy child with lots of issues, it is a very heavy burden to bear. The thing people need to realize is that this doesn't just happen by chance. It is rare that a set of parents did everything we discussed in this book and their child still turned out unhappy and plagued with problems.

Next, the simple truth is that there is nothing the average person can look back on and feel a greater sense of accomplishment from than raising a child correctly. When it comes our time to leave this life, we all have a legacy. For some it is small, for some it is large, and all are open to interpretation. If we do a good job raising our children, however, we can look in the mirror knowing we will leave the world a better place because we have provided the world with someone who will help push society forward, not drag it down. There are a few people who can honestly look at their other accomplishments and say they rival raising their children correctly, but not many. Everyone, however, who has a child has the opportunity to leave a positive legacy, and that's a wonderful opportunity we should not squander.

Finally we close with what it feels like to have your children look up to you and know that you helped them get to where they want to be. It is so gratifying to see your children achieve their goals, but words can't describe the feeling you get deep in your soul when your child demonstrates that they know that you are helping them. It could be a smile, a hug, or a thank you in front of the graduating class. For a parent, experiencing that feeling is indeed the finish line. I go back to what Michael Phelps said about his mom, which I am sure was ten times as gratifying for her as the eight gold medals. He said of him and his sisters, "We had a great mother raising us and we wouldn't trade her for anything. She's awesome...none of this could be done without her."

ADDITIONAL RESOURCES

Advocates for Highway Safety. *Studies Show Young Children at Risk in Auto Accidents.* Insure.com. www.insure.com/car-insurance/children-car-injuries.html (37).

Armour, Stephanie. *Generation Y: They've Arrived at Work With a New Attitude.* USA Today Online. www.usatoday.com/money/workplace/2005-11-06-gen-y_x.htm. (13).

Associated Press. *Almost 4 in 10 U.S. Children Born Out of Wedlock in 2005.* USA Today Online. www.usatoday.com/news/health/2006-11-21-births_x.htm. (11).

Baker, Jennifer L., Ph.D.; Lina W. Olsen, Ph.D.; and Thorkild I.A. Sørensen, M.D., Dr.Med.Sci. *Childhood Body-Mass Index and the Risk of Coronary Heart Disease in Adulthood.* The New England

Journal of Medicine. www.content.nejm.org/cgi/content/full/357/23/2329. (8).

Bodget, Henry. *Our Debt Problem Explained.* The Business Insider. www.businessinsider.com/henry-blodget-our-de-2009-4. (9).

Casner-Lotto, Jill. *Are They Really Ready to Work?* Partnership for 21st Century Skills. www.21stcenturyskills.org/documents/FINAL_REPORT_PDF09-29-06.pdf. (4).

Centers for Disease Control and Prevention. *Web-based Injury Statistics Query and Reporting System (WISQARS) (2008).* www.cdc.gov/ncipc/wisqars. (38).

Clark, Cheryl. *UCSD study: Kids' Physical Activity Drops off Between 9–15.* www.SignOnSanDiego.com. www.signonsandiego.com/news/health/20080715-1720-bn15physical.html. (30).

Clotfelter, Dr. John and Philip Cook. *The National Gambling Impact Study Commission, Final Report, June 1999.* 7 - 10. (10).

Community Partnership for Youth. *Standards.* www.CPY.org. www.cpy.org/standards.html. (40).

Council of Economic Advisers to the President. *Teens and Their Parents in the 21st Century: An Examination of Trends in Teen Behavior and the Role of Parental Involvement.* Education Resource Information Center. www.eric.ed.gov. (24).

Dairy Council of California. *More than Just Eating at Home.* Meals Matter. www.mealsmatter.org/ EatingForHealth/Topics/Healthy-Living-Articles/ Family-Meals.aspx. (23) and (26).

Elert, Glenn, ed. *Number of Televisions in the US.* The Physics Fact book. hypertextbook.com/facts/2007/ TamaraTamazashvili.shtml. (15)

Farkas, Steve and Jean Johnson. *Aggravating Circumstances.* Public Agenda. www.publicagenda. org/reports/aggravating-circumstances. (3).

Farner, Barbara. *Eating Out Healthy.* University of Illinois Extension- Your Health and You. www.urbanext.illinois.edu/yourhealth/default. cfm?IssueID=24. (14).

Freedman, D.S., W.H. Dietz, S.R. Srinivasan, and G.S. Berenson. *The Relation of Overweight to Cardiovascular Risk Factors among Children and Adolescents: The Bogalusa Heart Study.* Pediatrics. Vol. 103 No. 6 June 1999. (6).

Freeman, Robert. *Why Schools Are Failing: They Aren't;*
Parents Are. San Jose Mercury News. November 30,
2008. (34).

Gamerman, Ellen. *Bad Parents and Proud of It: Moms*
and a Dad Confess. The Wall Street Journal. April
19, 2009. (39).

Gillman, M.W., S.L. Rifas-Shiman, A.L. Frazier, H.R.H.
Rockette, C.A. Camargo, A.E. Field, C.S. Berkey,
and G.A. Colditz. *Family dinners and diet quality*
among older children and adolescents. Archives of
Family Medicine, 9,235-240. (25).

Hofferth, Sandra L. Curtin, Sally C. *Leisure Time*
Activities in Middle Childhood. Paper prepared for
the Positive Outcomes Conference, Washington,
DC, March 12-13, 2003. (22).

Institute of Education Science. *Highlights from the*
TIMSS. US Department of Education. nces.ed.gov/
pubSearch/pubsinfo.asp?pubid=2003011. (1).

Kaiser Family Foundation. *Generation M: Media in the*
Lives of 8–18 Year-Olds. www.kff.org/entmedia/
entmedia030905pkg.cfm. (29).

Kelly, Michael. *Study Finds Children Reading Less for*
Fun. www.SignOnSanDiego.com. (Accessed June
28, 2008). (35).

Kutler, Lawrence, Ph.D. *Playing One Parent against Another.* www.drkutner.com/parenting/articles/playing.html. (18).

La Fontana, Kathryn M., Ph.D. *Majority of Americans Cite Sense of Entitlement Among Youth.* www.sacredheart.edu/pages/28154_majority_of_americans_cite_sense_of_entitlement_among_youth_says_national_poll.cfm. (12).

LimiTV Staff. *Information- Effects of TV.* www.limitv.org/news_articles.htm. (28).

Ludwig, David S., M.D., Ph.D. *Child Obesity - The Shape of Things to Come.* The New England Journal of Medicine. content.nejm.org/cgi/content/full/357/23/2325. (7).

Michigan Department of Education. *What Research Says About Parent Involvment in Children's Education.* www.michigan.gov/documents/Final_Parent_Involvement_Fact_Sheet_14732_7.pdf. (32) and (33).

Monster.com. *On the Road Again - Americans Willing to Relocate for Work.* about-monster.com/content/road-again-americans-willing-relocate-work-monster-releases-job-seeker-mobility-data-analysi. (17).

Mrowka, Marcus. "McDonalds Sued for Making Children Obese." *The GW Hatchet*. November 25, 2002. (20).

Mullis, Dr. Ina V.S. and Dr. Michael O. Martin. *Overview of PIRLS 2006 Results.* www.iea.nl/fileadmin/user_upload/PIRLS2006/Overview_Results.pdf. (2).

National Center for Health Statistics. *NHANES_data on the Prevalence of Overweight among Children and Adolescents: United States, 2003–2004.* Centers for Disease Control and Prevention. www.cdc.gov/nchs/data/hestat/overweight/overwght_child_03.htm. (5).

National Center for Substance Abuse (CASA) at Columbia University. *The Importance of Family Dinners IV.* www.casacolumbia.org/templates/publications_reports.aspx. (27).

National Reading Panel. *Teaching Children to Read - Summary Report.* www.nationalreadingpanel.org/Publications/summary.htm. (36).

Office of External Affairs. *Let's Go Outside!* U.S. Fish and Wildlife Service. www.fws.gov/letsgooutside/. (31).

Tanner, Lindsey. *1 in 5 kids get little vitamin D, study says. Washington Post.* www.washingtonpost.com/wp-dyn/content/article/2009/10/26/AR2009102600858.html?sub=AR. (19).

US Department of Transportation. *Licensed Drivers and Vehicles Registrations.* www.fhwa.dot.gov/. (16).

Zeratsky, Katherine, R.D., L.D. *High-Fructose Corn Syrup: Why Is It So Bad for Me?* medicineinfobiz.com/health/high-fructose-corn-syrup/AN01588.htm. (21).

ABOUT THE AUTHOR

John McPherson is a leadership and management consultant in Salinas, CA. He and his wife, Christina, have two children who keep them on their toes.

LaVergne, TN USA
14 January 2010
169944LV00001B/15/P